SCHOOL COUNSELOR

because

awesome

MULTITASKING

NINJA

ISN'T A REAL

job title

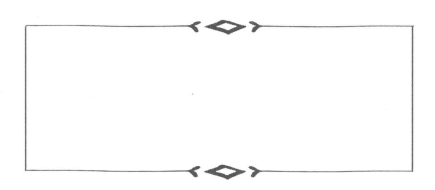

True happiness is to enjoy the present without anxious dependence upon the future.

— Seneca

This above all: to thine ownself be true.

— Shakespeare

Excellence is not an act, but a habit.

– Aristotle

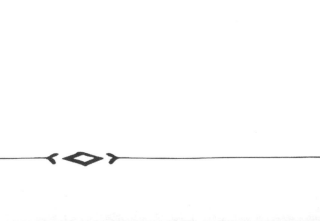

No act of kindness, no matter how small, is ever wasted.

— Aesop

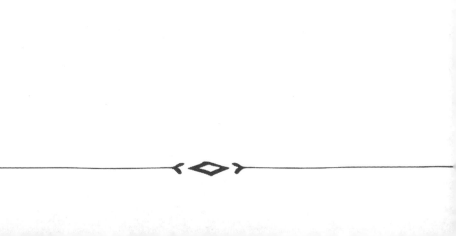

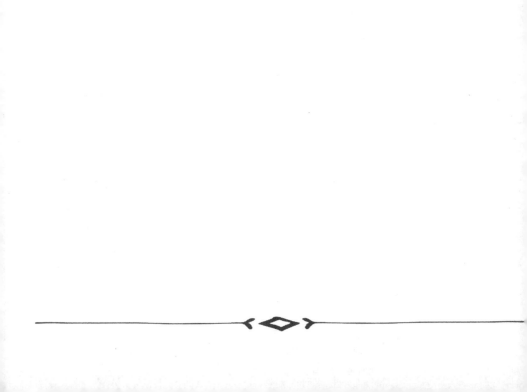

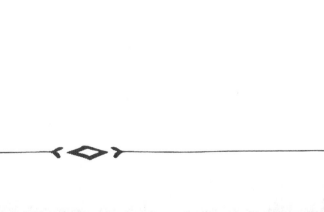

The way to be happy is to make others so.

– Robert Ingersoll

We know what we are now, but
not what we may become.

- Shakespeare

Life is not a problem to be solved,
but a reality to be experienced.

— PJ Bailey

I am not bothered by the fact that I am not understood.

— Confucius

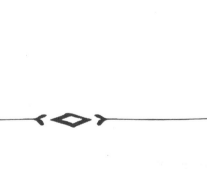

The greatest mistake you can make in life is
to be continually fearing you will make one.

– Elbert Hubbard

Made in the USA
Columbia, SC
09 December 2021

50879360R00054